batman :: cacophony

KEVIN SMITH
writer

WALT FLANAGAN
penciller

SANDRA HOPE
inker

GUY MAJOR
colorist

JARED K. FLETCHER
letterer

BATMAN *created by Bob Kane*

DAN DIDIO :: SVP-EXECUTIVE EDITOR & EDITOR-ORIGINAL SERIES
GEORG BREWER :: VP-DESIGN & DC DIRECT CREATIVE
BOB HARRAS :: GROUP EDITOR-COLLECTED EDITIONS
SEAN MACKIEWICZ :: EDITOR
ROBBIN BROSTERMAN :: DESIGN DIRECTOR-BOOKS

DC COMICS
PAUL LEVITZ :: PRESIDENT & PUBLISHER
RICHARD BRUNING :: SVP-CREATIVE DIRECTOR
PATRICK CALDON :: EVP-FINANCE & OPERATIONS
AMY GENKINS :: SVP-BUSINESS & LEGAL AFFAIRS
JIM LEE :: EDITORIAL DIRECTOR-WILDSTORM
GREGORY NOVECK :: SVP-CREATIVE AFFAIRS
STEVE ROTTERDAM :: SVP-SALES & MARKETING
CHERYL RUBIN :: SVP-BRAND MANAGEMENT

Cover by Adam Kubert
Publication design by Robbie Biederman

SUSTAINABLE
FORESTRY
INITIATIVE

Certified Chain of Custody
Promoting Sustainable
Forest Management
www.sfiprogram.org

Fiber used in this product line meets the
sourcing requirements of the SFI program.
www.sfiprogram org NFS SPIC0C C0001801

introduction by KEVIN SMITH

To address the elephant in the room, yes — Walt got the job because he's my friend. And, yes — it's unseemly and unprofessional to trade in such naked nepotism; so much so that a base-coach from the *other* team insinuated that I bullied DC editorial into giving my guy the job.

I mean, sure — that's *one* way to look at it. Or you can view it through *this* prism: without Walt, not only would "Cacophony" not exist, I'd have likely never read any comics beyond *Sad Sack* or *Hot Stuff the L'il Devil*.

Walt Flanagan was my comics guru. Circa 1989, we worked together at the Highlands Recreation Center for a year, during which time he'd loan me copies of THE DARK KNIGHT RETURNS, WATCHMEN and *Mage*.

It was an age of wonders. We'd spend weekends going to Fred Greenberg's NY comic book shows at the Penn Hotel, cherry picking the wall books and discount boxes 'til dusk — at which point, we two suburbanite lads would scamper back home to Monmouth County, where nobody's ever been mugged. When there wasn't a weekend show to hit, we'd drive from one end of Jersey to the other with a phone book, tracking down hole-in-the-wall hobby shops, hoping to find still-racked, first printings of THE KILLING JOKE (re: phonebook — mind you, this is in the pre-internet, pre-GPS, nearly-crustacean era).

Walt Flanagan always liked to draw. He had a penchant for drawing Metal-influenced zombies.

During those many hours on toll roads, we'd talk about the story arcs and specific issues we loved, and — like all comic fans — how we would've improved plot points or dialogue with our fan-boy attention to detail and love of continuity. And after all that unwitting training, a decade or so later, I was actually writing for those very DC characters I'd rhapsodized about with Walt while trekking up and down the state, looking for new wall books at old rack prices.

No slouch himself, Walt had teamed up with his cinematic and real world best-y, Bryan Johnson, to create both *Karney* and *War of the Undead* for IDW. The most involvement I had with either mini was an intro I did for the *Karney* trade.

So there we were: two comics-lovin' dudes from the Jersey 'burbs who both fulfilled dreams of making funny books.

But we'd never done it *together* (y'know, a comic book; not "whoopee").

And that's what I was thinking when I saw the "Dark Knight" billboard.

Oh, I was always a Batman fan: from a childhood of afternoons spent watching Adam West "Batman" reruns when school let out, to Tim Burton's groundbreaking film in '89, to everything Marshall Rogers and Frank Miller had ever done that featured the cowled crusader. But the teaser trailers for Nolan's flick? The billboards? It reignited my Bat-thusiasm. I fell in love all over again.

Confession time: I haven't read weekly new books in over five years. I fell behind in my reading, then fell even further behind, then stopped reading altogether. Walt would keep me updated as to what was happening in the various plotlines of the many titles I used to regularly read. I'd long since lost the desire to write comics — largely because I'd become *persona non grata* in the comics community, due to my incessant lateness. But looking up at that billboard? I became very interested in Batman again. And the more I stared at the billboard, the more I "saw" Walt's name.

Here was one of my closest friends in the world — the guy responsible for my four-color enthusiasm — drawing comics. Here was me, wanting to write some comics. And neither of us were getting any younger.

So I called Dan DiDio, who I'd met many years prior, and asked him if I could write a Batman mini and have my longtime friend draw it. Dan understood immediately that my passion for the project was being fueled by the desire to bring my comics interest full circle: create a miniseries *with* my comics-brother-from-another-mother handling the art chores.

And man, was it fun for us — not to mention a dream come true.

Fun and educational, actually. I banged out the first two scripts in a week, but it wasn't until issue one streeted that I did a second draft — all thanks to a CACOPHONY review in which a critic pointed out that some of the dialogue I'd given Batman didn't sound natural in the least when spoken aloud. I gave it a test run and the blogger was absolutely correct: I'd gotten too showy with the word balloons. So I re-drafted all the dialogue for the next two issues, scraping away the excess verbiage, and boiling each sentiment down to the same Bat-time (same Bat-channel).

On the art front, Walt would draw a rough of the page. If necessary, I'd ask for tweaks, then he'd take it to full pencils. And over the course of three issues, both of us got better at creating a comic book. The writing improved from issue one to issue three, and the art followed suit (indeed, peep out the "Fountainhead" reading sequences in issue one and three; they look like they were drawn by two different artists entirely).

So for those who'd snark about me getting my friend a job: you've got it all wrong. Scrape away everything else, and you'll see that *I'M* the friend who benefited from nepotism; because if it weren't for Walt Flanagan, I wouldn't have this gig. Walt is Batman himself — and me? I've always been nothing more than a fat-and-flabby, immature, over-eager Robin.

But to be fair, once we got the approval from Dan and DC, I started thinking about how I'd written Batman into a bit of my GREEN ARROW run, yet said in many an interview, "I don't wanna write a Batman story ever; it's fun to use him as a supporting player instead." What a stupid thing to say. Why limit yourself when it came to the single most interesting superhero ever created? Why not try to write the best Batman story you could?

No – that's *not* CACOPHONY.

By series' end, I realized it wasn't the best Batman story I could write; nor was it Walt's finest hour. By the time we were finished, I saw CACOPHONY for what it was: a dress rehearsal for the best Batman story I could write/ Walt could draw. It was a warm-up. Quentin Tarantino (yeah, I'm dropping names) once told me that he wanted to do another martial arts flick after the *Kill Bill* films because by the time those flicks were done, he'd learned how to do it. His logic was "Now I've got all this expertise in the field. Why not put it to use immediately?"

So the three issues of CACOPHONY gave birth to a twelve-issue maxi-series that Walt and I are working on now, for release this fall. Entitled BATMAN: THE WIDENING GYRE, it is, for sure, the *best* Batman story either of us can do.

Meantime, 'til that hits the stands? Please enjoy the *second*-best Batman story me and Walt could tell.

Kevin Smith
6/22/09

batman ::cacophony #1 *cover by* ADAM KUBERT

LONGTIME FRONT GATE GUARDS SAM JENNINGS AND ROY KELLY WERE FORCED TO LOOK FOR WORK IN A JOB MARKET THAT HAS LITTLE USE FOR EMPLOYEES OVER FIFTY.

WHEN HIS UNEMPLOYMENT BENEFITS RAN OUT SAM FILED FOR GOVERNMENT ASSISTANCE.

HIS WIFE--NOW FORCED TO USE FOOD STAMPS AT THEIR NEIGHBORHOO. SUPERMARKET-- REGULARLY BERATES SAM FOR BRINGING HER SO LOW.

ROY, HOWEVER--ALWAYS THE MORE INDUSTRIOUS OF THE TWO--TOOK OUT AN AD IN THE GOTHAM GAZETTE'S PERSONALS SECTION THAT RAN EVERY DAY FOR TWO MONTHS.

PAF!

"FORMER ARKHAM SECURITY GUARD SEEKS EMPLOYMENT OR OTHER" THE LISTING READ.

"THIRTY YEARS' EXPERIENCE IN THE WORLD'S MOST DANGEROUS AND SECURE PENAL INSTITUTION. INQUIRIES CONTACT BOX 1145"

LAST WEEK, HE FINALLY GOT THE CALL HE'D HOPED WOULD EVENTUALLY COME.

TWO DAYS AGO, ROY SOLD THIRTY YEARS' WORTH OF ARKHAM ACCESS CODES, SHIFT DETAILS, FLOOR PLANS, AND VARIOUS OTHER INSIDER KNOWLEDGE OF THE ASYLUM FOR TWENTY THOUSAND DOLLARS.

ROY USED HIS EARNINGS TO MOVE TO BAJA, MEXICO.

HE PLANS TO OPEN A BEACH-FRONT MOPED RENTAL OPERATION AND SPEND THE PROFITS ON BOOZE AND LOOSE WOMEN FOR THE REMAINDER OF HIS DAYS.

'LO, FLOYD.

JOKER.

IF I'D KNOWN YOU WERE COMING, I'D'VE DONE MY HAIR. OR AT LEAST PUT ON MY MERKIN.

I'VE GOT A GREEN ONE, NATCH. THE CURTAINS HAVE TO MATCH THE DRAPES, AS THEY SAY.

HEH.

THEY'VE GOT YOU LOCKED UP GOOD AND TIGHT, HUH?

THIS IS THE SAME STUFF THEY MADE THE POPE-MOBILE OUT OF, I'M TOLD--ONLY THICKER.

I MISS THE BARS. BUT THROW ONE MEASLY PIECE OF POO AT A GUARD, AND SUDDENLY IT'S ALL BULLET-PROOF GLASS FOR OUR HERO.

'COURSE, THE POO DID HAVE RAZOR BLADES IN IT, BUT STILL.

TO WHAT DO I OWE THE PLEASURE OF THIS LATE-NIGHT POP-IN?

...AS THAT LIKE "MAX, WORTH"? 'CAUSE I NEVER READ THAT SOAP-OPERA-Y CRAP.

"FOR BETTER OR FOR WORSE" GRINDS MY GEARS, TOO.

S'NOT A COMIC. MAXIE ZEUS--THE *CRIME* LORD.

WAIT--YOU MEAN THE *LAMEST* BOSS IN THE GOTHAM UNDERWORLD?

THAT'S THE ONE.

WELL, HE FOUND AN OLD CACHE OF YOUR JOKER VENOM LAST TIME YOU GOT PUT AWAY AND STARTED CUTTING IT WITH *ECSTASY.*

THEY CALL IT "CHUCKLES"--ON ACCOUNT OF IT'S A *GIGGLY* HIGH, TOO, APPARENTLY. PEOPLE LOVE A DRUG THAT MAKES 'EM STUPID.

STUFF CAUGHT ON IN THE *CLUBS* FIRST, THEN SPREAD OUT INTO THE *SUBURBS.* SIDE EFFECTS ARE PRETTY *NASTY* AS YOU MIGHT IMAGINE: LOCKJAW, PARANOIA, PSYCHOSIS. BUT WHEN'VE DANGEROUS *SIDE EFFECTS* EVER STOPPED FOLKS FROM DOING DRUGS?

IT'S BECOME PRETTY *POPULAR*--AT LEAST IN GOTHAM. LAST MONTH, *TIME* CALLED IT "THE WORST DRUG EPIDEMIC SINCE CRACK IN THE LATE '80s."

WHAT?!

APPARENTLY, IF YOU *DILUTE* THE DOSAGE, YOUR POISON GIVES A GREAT HIGH.

NOW *THAT* IS CLASSIC JOKER RIGHT THERE: A GUY'S MAKING A *FORTUNE* OFF SOME POISON YOU CREATED...

THAT *TWO-BIT* CARPETBAGGER! HE'S RUINING MY GOOD NAME!

AND WHAT'S BUGGING YOU THE MOST IS THAT PEOPLE'RE GETTING AN UNHEALTHY *KICK* FROM YOUR POISON NOW, INSTEAD OF DROPPING *DEAD* INSTANTLY.

"GOOD"?

JOKER VENOM'S SUPPOSED TO BE FEARED, NOT "*ROCKED*" AT A "*KEGGER*"!

IF IT'S ANY CONSOLATION, SOME FOLKS ARE OVERDOSING ON "CHUCKLES" TOO. SO, Y'KNOW-- YOU'RE *STILL* KINDA RACKING UP THE BODY COUNT.

I'LL *KILL* HIM!

HA. YOU ARE A COMEDIAN.

DO ME A SOLID AND STEP AWAY FROM THE GLASS, PLEASE. I WANT YOU IN ONE PIECE WHEN I EMPTY TWO CLIPS IN YOUR HEAD.

OH...

JUST DO ME A FAVOR AND DON'T EVER TELL *TETCH*.

SHHHHHH...

THAT *MIDGET'S* BEEN TRYING TO GET ME TO DO THIS FOR YEARS NOW, AND I TOLD HIM I DON'T *SWING* THAT...

HUH?

HEY! WHERE'D YOU GO?!

SEDUCED AND ABANDONED.

"I FEEL SO *DIRTY*..."

SOFILTHYSICK ANDDIRTY...

PURITYFROMRELEASE OFBANALLIVESTHEY SHOULDBETHANKINGME NOTJUDGINGMEWITH THEIRCLERGYEYES...

CAN'TCLEANSETHEIR SINSITWITHOUTTHE GLASSESANYMORETHE GLASSESSOICANSEE MYSELFREFLECTEDIN THEIRARTIFICIALGAZES...

BEGGINGMETO BAPTISETHEM ANEWINTHE LITURGYOFTHEKNIFE ANDBLOOD...

No--not just VICTIMS. PEOPLE.

Two people who somehow found one another in an otherwise horrible world.

Like my PARENTS.

Oh no...

Parents...

CHILDREN!

No more marks tonight, Zsasz.

I swear.

FLY AWAY, BATMAN!

YOU HEAR ME?! GET OUTA HERE OR I SEND THESE KIDS TO MEET THEIR PARENTS!

MOMMY!

I'M JUST FIBBING TO HIM, KID. I'VE GOTTA KILL YOU AND YOUR SISTER. ONLY 'CAUSE I LOVE YOU SO MUCH.

THIS'LL ONLY STING FOR A SECOND...

EEEEK!

KRUNCH

HYUCK!

AHHHH!

28

The monster can't hurt you now.

ZSASZ IS RESTRAINED ON THE SECOND FLOOR. HE'LL REQUIRE MEDICAL ATTENTION.

SEE THAT HE DOESN'T GET IT FOR AT LEAST AN HOUR.

THE COMMISSIONER'S LOOKING FOR YOU, SIR.

HE SAID TO TELL YOU...

COMING THROUGH! MAKE A HOLE!

"CODE GREEN."

Not AGAIN.

ARKHAM ASYLUM

GCPD

HAPPENED ABOUT AN HOUR AGO. NO SIGN OF HIM. WE DON'T KNOW HOW HE GOT OUT YET.

HOW MANY DEAD?

THAT'S THE THING: *NOBODY'S* DEAD. WELL, EXCEPT ONE. WE'VE GOT ABOUT A DOZEN GUARDS AND PERSONNEL SHOT UP WITH TRANQUILIZER DARTS AND DEADSHOT'S BODY.

BODY?

YEAH. LOOKS LIKE SOMEBODY BLEW HIS BRAINS OUT.

NEAREST WE CAN FIGURE IS DEADSHOT BROKE IN TO BUST THE CLOWN OUT, AND THEN THE JOKER TURNED ON HIM.

WHERE'S DEADSHOT?

"THEY JUST LOADED HIM INTO THE MEAT WAGON. M.E. TRIED TO GET HIS OUTFIT OFF HIM, BUT IT'S RIGGED WITH SOME KINDA SEALANT.

AMBULANCE

AMBULANCE

GOTHAM CITY EMERGENCY SQUAD

721

"THEY'RE GONNA TRY TO CUT HIM OUT OF HIS COSTUME AT THE MORGUE FOR THE AUTOPSY."

ZZZz

ZZZZiip

UHN...

LAWTON.

30

A WEEK LATER...

PUNY MORTAL! HAVE YOU NO FAITH IN YOUR *GOD*?!

BEHOLD THE DIVINE POWER *OF* THE MIGHTY ZEUS!

IS *THIS* YOUR CARD?

THAT *WAS* MY CARD!

HA-HA. AND *THAT'S* ABOUT THE EXTENT OF MY "GODLY POWERS" NOW.

SO WE'VE SEEN THE *END* OF THE *TOGA*-WEARING MAXIE ZEUS THEN?

OH, YES. NO MORE SANDALS FOR ME. IT'S ONLY EIGHTEEN HUNDRED DOLLAR *BERLUTIS* FROM HERE ON OUT.

LOOK, I GET IT: I'VE HAD SOME PRETTY *PUBLIC* EXTENDED PSYCHOLOGICAL BREAK-DOWNS. I CAN'T HIDE FROM THE FACT THAT EVERY NEWS STATION IN TOWN HAS FOOTAGE OF ME RUNNING AROUND LOOKING LIKE LOOKING LIKE BRAD PITT IN "TROY".

BUT THAT'S ALL BEHIND ME NOW. TWO YEARS AGO, I FINALLY GOT THE HELP I NEEDED. I'M ON PRESCRIBED MEDICATION TO STABILIZE MY DIAGNOSED BIPOLAR DISORDER. THE DEMENTIA'S GONE, THE ILLUSIONS OF GRANDEUR ARE GONE.

I'VE PAID MY DEBTS TO SOCIETY, SO TO SPEAK, AND NOW I JUST WANNA CONTINUE BUILDING THE COMPANY I LET SLIP AWAY WHILE I WAS BATTLING MENTAL ILLNESS.

MAXIE ZEUS IS DEAD, BUT *MAXIMILIAN* ZEUS-- THE SHIPPING MAGNATE WITH THE *LEGITIMATE* BUSINESS--IS VERY MUCH ALIVE AND *WELL*.

SOME HAVE SUGGESTED THAT NOT ALL OF YOUR BUSINESS VENTURES ARE LEGITIMATE, MR. ZEUS. HOW DO YOU ADDRESS THE ACCUSATIONS THAT YOU'RE BEHIND THE MULTIMILLION-DOLLAR "CHUCKLES" EPIDEMIC?

I THINK IT'S TRAGIC THAT IN THIS, THE TWENTY-FIRST CENTURY, THERE'S *STILL* RAMPANT ETHNIC DISCRIMINATION. I'M A *GREEK*--A *FOREIGNER*--SO NATURALLY, I *MUST* BE UP TO NO GOOD.

AS LONG AS OLD WHITE MEN RUN THIS COUNTRY, THE POLITICIANS AND THE MEDIA WILL *ALWAYS* OFFER UP A BOGEYMAN WITH AN *ACCENT* OR A DARKER *SKIN TONE* AS THE SCAPEGOAT FOR EVERY PROBLEM THEY CAN'T OR WON'T FIX THEMSELVES.

THEY FOSTER MISTRUST AND HATRED, RATHER THAN UNITY, BECAUSE THEY HAVE TO FUEL *FEAR*, YOU SEE--SO THEY CAN KEEP ALL OF US FROM ADDRESSING THE *REAL* PROBLEMS AT THE VOTING BOOTHS.

OCCAM'S RAZOR TELLS US THAT THE *SIMPLEST* SOLUTION IS ALWAYS THE BEST, YES?

WELL, BASED ON THAT, WHO DO YOU *THINK* IS BEHIND A DESIGNER DRUG SYNTHESIZED FROM A TOXIN CREATED BY THE *JOKER?*

WHAT WILL YOU DO TO DISPEL THE RUMORS THAT YOU'RE THE "CHUCKLES" MASTERMIND, THEN?

ALL I CAN DO IS MAKE THE DIFFERENCES I CAN *MAKE*--TO SHOW GOTHAM, AND THE WORLD, THAT I'M NOT A *DRUG* LORD; I'M A *PHILANTHROPIST.*

THAT'S WHY I FUNDED THE *PARTHENON*-- THE STATE-OF-THE-ART ELEMENTARY SCHOOL IN MIDTOWN. *PRIVATE* SCHOOL EDUCATIONS AT *PUBLIC* SCHOOL PRICES. MY *NEPHEW* EVEN GOES THERE!

WE'RE BUILDING SHARP, YOUNG MINDS WHO'LL GROW UP AND CHANGE THE SYSTEM ONE DAY. WHEN THESE KIDS ARE ADULTS, THEY'LL MAKE *RACISM* AND *FEAR- MONGERING* A THING OF THE PAST--YOU *WATCH.*

WHAT'RE YOU *CRAZY?* I'M IN THE MIDDLE OF...

OH GOD, NO.

WE'RE GONNA HAVE TO CUT THIS *SHORT,* MISS.

OH. UH--WE STILL DIDN'T GET TO THE TALK ABOUT *OLYMPUS* AND WHAT A HOT-SPOT IT'S BECOME.

YES, YES. I'M SORRY--WE'VE JUST HAD SOMETHING COME UP THAT *DEMANDS* MY *IMMEDIATE* ATTENTION. KOSTAS WILL SHOW YOU OUT.

A SPEEDY EXIT FROM OLYMPUS...

VVWRRRMMM

GDCMPLX

A SPEEDIER ARRIVAL AT MAXIE'S PARTHENON SCHOOL...

SCREEEEECH

MPLX

36

PLEASE, JOKER...
DON'T HURT THE KIDS...
OH, THAT'S RICH, COMING FROM THE DRUG PEDDLER.
RUN ALONG NOW, LI'L AESOP. I'VE GOTTA HAVE A WORD WITH YOUR UNCLE.
WHAT'S THE BIG IDEA, YOU THIEVING, OILY GOAT-LOVER?!
NOW TAKE IT EASY, JOKER...
I'M GONNA TAKE IT ALL, ONASSIS! STARTING WITH YOUR WORTHLESS, BIPOLAR HIDE!
A MAN WORKS HIS WHOLE LIFE TO BUILD A REPUTATION FOR MAYHEM AND MURDER, AND THEN SOME TWO-BIT WANNABE HOOD WITH THE WORST GIMMICK THIS SIDE OF CALENDAR MAN CHEAPENS HIS BEST EFFORTS TO LEAVE BEHIND A LEGACY!
Whoooo's in our class?
Edgar
Bryan
Michael
"OH, I KNOW! I'LL MAKE YET ANOTHER DOPEY DESIGNER DRUG TO GOOFY-UP THE MASSES, BECAUSE NOBODY'S EVER THOUGHT OF SOMETHING LIKE THAT BEFORE UH-DOYYYYYY!"
PANT PANT PANT
WHAT WAS THE PLAN?
WHAT EXACTLY DID I SAY TO YOU BEFORE THEY LOCKED ME UP IN CAMP HAPPY THE LAST TIME?
YOU ASKED ME TO RANDOMLY JOKERIZE GOTHAMITES ON APRIL FIRST SO THAT BATMAN WOULD PUZZLE OVER WHETHER YOU WERE AT LARGE OR NOT AND BE FORCED TO COME TO ARKHAM TO SEE YOU.
AT WHICH TIME...?
AT WHICH TIME YOU WERE GONNA SAY "APRIL FOOLS" TO HIM.

SIMPLE INSTRUCTIONS, MAXIE. VERY SIMPLE. AMYGDALA COULD'VE FOLLOWED THOSE INSTRUCTIONS.

BUT APRIL FOOL'S DAY CAME AND WENT, AND GUESS WHAT? I GOT *NO* VISIT FROM THE *BAT!* INSTEAD OF DOING LIKE I ASKED, YOU WENT AND TURNED YOURSELF INTO *SCARFACE!*

THE AL *PACINO* SCARFACE, NOT THE GUY WITH THE PUPPET.

I KNOW. AND FOR RUINING YOUR APRIL FOOL'S DAY PRANK, I'M *SORRY. TRULY.*

BUT JOKER, C'MON--THIS IS SO MUCH *BETTER!* WE'VE GOT AN *EMPIRE* NOW-- WITH A LEGITIMATE *FACE!* AND HALF OF THAT IS *YOURS!*

OH, MAXIE.

MAXIE, MAXIE, MAXIE...

WALK WITH ME, MY SOUVLAKI-SLURPING FRIEND.

I DON'T *WANT* AN EMPIRE, BUDDY. NEVER DID. ALL I WANT...

ALL I'VE *EVER* WANTED...

IS TO HAVE A GOOD TIME.

AND TO *ANNOY* BATMAN, WHENEVER POSSIBLE, OF COURSE.

AND TO ONE DAY *MURDER* BATMAN AND DEFILE HIS CARCASS SEXUALLY.

AND A *PONY.*

SO ALL THE *MONEY* YOU'RE MAKING OFF MY CREATION DOESN'T INTEREST ME. THE *POWER,* THE GLORY, THE *LEGITIMACY* THAT SEEMS TO MAKE YOU FEEL LIKE SUCH A BIG BOY?

I DON'T GIVE A RAT'S ASS ABOUT THAT STUFF.

SO I GUESS WHAT I'M SAYING IS...

WELL, YOU'RE NOT MY FRIEND ANYMORE.

WHICH MEANS WE HAVE A *GANG WAR* ON OUR HANDS.

HA HA HA.

OH, JOKER-- YOU ARE A FUNNY GUY.

WITH ALL DUE *RESPECT,* MY OLD FRIEND--YOU DON'T WANNA GO TO WAR WITH ME NOW. I'LL CRUSH YOU LIKE A *BUG.*

batman::cacophony #2 *cover by* ADAM KUBERT

AS IN EVERY MAJOR CITY, FRIDAY NIGHTS IN GOTHAM BELONG TO THE CLUB CROWD.

EVEN IN THE MIDST OF A CITYWIDE GANG WAR BETWEEN THIS CLUB'S OWNER--MAXIE ZEUS--AND THE URBAN TERRORIST KNOWN ONLY AS THE JOKER, GOTHAMITES SHRUG OFF ANY POSSIBLE THREAT TO THEIR WELL-BEING IN FAVOR OF SURRENDERING TO THE LESSER NATURE OF THEIR ANGELS.

COCAINE AND SPEED FIND NO TAKERS IN CLUB OLYMPUS LATELY. "CHUCKLES"--THE METHAMPHETAMINE DERIVED FROM THE JOKER'S OWN "VENOM"--RULES THE DAY.

THAT IT'S MANUFACTURED AND DISTRIBUTED BY THE CLUB'S OWNER DOESN'T DICTATE THE DEMAND; GOTHAM IS IN THE THROES OF A LOVE AFFAIR WITH "CHUCKLES."

BUT IT'S NOT JUST "CHUCKLES" THAT'S DRAWING THE CROWD TONIGHT. WORLD-RENOWNED DJ MITE IS BACK IN TOWN AFTER A MASSIVE EUROPEAN TOUR.

AND GOTHAM WILL ALWAYS CELEBRATE ITS OWN...

ESPECIALLY IF THEY DROP THE PHAT BEATS AND SPORT A GIMMICKY COSTUME.

WHAT THE ADORING, INEBRIATED CROWD DOESN'T KNOW IS THAT DJ MITE'S BODY WAS JUST FOUND IN HIS HOTEL BATHROOM BY A MAID WHO CAME FOR TURN-DOWN SERVICE.

HIS HEAD WAS LOCATED A HALF HOUR LATER BY THE POLICE, STUFFED IN THE MINI-BAR.

CLICK

ANOTHER OF GOTHAM'S *UPSTANDING* CITIZENS?

THIS ONE'S NOT *GOTHAM*-BASED. I DON'T KNOW *WHO* HE IS. ALL I'VE GOT ON HIM IS THAT HE TRIED TO *KILL* CONNOR HAWKE, THE SECOND *GREEN ARROW.*

FURTHER PROOF THAT NO *LEAGUER* SHOULD EVER LET SOMEONE *ELSE* ASSUME THEIR *MANTLE.*

I'M SURE *JEAN PAUL VALLEY* WOULD BE HEARTBROKEN TO HEAR YOU SAY THAT, SIR.

FUNNY.

Harrisburg Times
BUCKEYE HONORED BY CITY
HARRISBURG CRIMEFIGHTER IS GIVEN A HERO'S RECEPTION

HE ALSO KILLED TWO LESSER-KNOWN *VIGILANTES* IN PENNSYLVANIA.

SO *SOMEONE* HAS A FILE ON HIM, THEN, THAT WOULD INCLUDE HIS *IDENTITY* OR AT LEAST A *NAME?*

NO--I PUT THAT TOGETHER MYSELF, WHEN I MATCHED THE BALLISTICS IN THE KILLINGS OF VIRAGO AND BUCKEYE TO THE SLUGS THEY PULLED FROM CONNOR.

HOW DID YOU ACCESS THE CONNOR HAWKE *SLUGS?*

I *LIBERATED* THEM FROM STAR CITY GENERAL SHORTLY AFTER THE INCIDENT.

YOU MOST *DEFINITELY* NEED A *HOBBY,* MASTER BRUCE.

SO WE'RE TO ASSUME, THEN, THAT THE JOKER IS IN *COLLUSION* WITH THIS *HERO-KILLER?*

I'M NOT SURE. WE *COULD* JUST VIEW HIS SUDDEN APPEARANCE AT THE CLUB AS NOTHING MORE THAN FORTUITOUS TIMING FROM WHICH THE JOKER BENEFITED.

BUT IF HE MATCHES THE *DESCRIPTION* DEADSHOT GAVE YOU FROM THE ARKHAM BREAK-IN AND HE STOPPED YOU FROM PUTTING DOWN THE JOKER THIS EVENING, WE *MUST* SURMISE THE PAIR ARE *WORKING TOGETHER,* DO WE NOT?

I'VE GOT ANOTHER THEORY, ALFRED.

WHAT DO VIRAGO, BUCKEYE, GREEN ARROW AND I HAVE IN COMMON?

MINOR *PSYCHOSES* AND *GOD COMPLEXES,* SIR?

WE'RE ALL *NON-METAHUMANS,* COMMITTED TO THE FIGHT FOR JUSTICE. IF YOU HARBORED *FANTASIES* OF *HERO-KILLING,* YOU'D HAVE LITTLE HOPE OF TAKING DOWN *SUPERMAN* OR *WONDER WOMAN.*

BUT A NORMAL PERSON SUCH AS *YOURSELF,* SIR...

AND I USE THE TERM "NORMAL" *VERY* LOOSELY...

...WOULD MAKE FOR A *CONCEIVABLE* TARGET.

EXACTLY.

EVERYONE KNOWS THAT, WHEN THE JOKER'S AT LARGE, I'LL CONCENTRATE ALL MY EFFORTS ON *APPREHENDING* HIM.

SO MAYBE BREAKING THE JOKER OUT OF *ARKHAM* WAS THIS MANIAC'S WAY OF *DANGLING BAIT.*

I WANT YOU TO KEEP *TIM* AS FAR *AWAY* FROM THIS AS POSSIBLE, ALFRED. KEEP HIM IN THE *DARK* ON THIS ONE. BECAUSE IF MY THEORY IS CORRECT...

I'M BEING *HUNTED.*

WE LIVE ONLY TO SERVE A GOD.

AND OTHER STUFF, TOO. ≶GIGGLE≷

LET US FILL THY MOUTH WITH GRAPES...

COME JOIN US, OH MIGHTY ZEUS...

KOSTAS, TAKE THY LEAVE OF ME, THAT I MIGHT INDULGE THESE VIRGINS WITH THE POWER OF ZEUS!

HOW DOST THOU WISH THE MIGHTY ZEUS TO LIE WITH THEE, LADIES?

IN THE FORM OF A BULL? A SWAN?

AS YOU WISH, MY LORD.

I'VE GOTTA GET HIM BACK ON THE THORAZINE.

C'MON. WE'RE TAKING THE BOYS OUT AND TURNING OVER EVERY RAT-HOLE IN THIS TOWN 'TIL WE FIND THE JOKER.

BUT WHAT ABOUT MAXIE?

HE'S FINE. GUY'LL GRIND HIS GEARS FOR AWHILE AND SLEEP 'TIL MORNING. PHIL AND TOM ARE ON THE BALCONY, SO THE PLACE IS COVERED.

...IS IN CUSTODY TONIGHT, AFTER HAVING SURRENDERED HIMSELF TO GOTHAM POLICE.

THE FORMER SHIPPING MAGNATE HAS CONFESSED TO BEING THE MASTERMIND BEHIND THE DEADLY DESIGNER DRUG "CHUCKLES"--

THE IMPETUS FOR THE CITY'S RECENT GANG WAR BETWEEN ZEUS AND THE URBAN TERRORIST KNOWN ONLY AS THE JOKER.

THAT CHICKEN-HEARTED PIECE'A POO!

AND WHEN DID THIS "URBAN TERRORIST" CRAP START? WHAT HAPPENED TO "SUPER-VILLAIN"?

ZEUS WILL BE HELD IN POLICE CUSTODY UNTIL HE'S TURNED OVER TO THE DEPARTMENT OF HOMELAND SECURITY FOR DEBRIEFING ON HIS AL QAEDA CONTACTS IN THE INTERNATIONAL DRUG TRADE.

WHAT?! THE FEDS?!?

I'M STUCK HERE IN ONE OF CLAYFACE'S OLD SAFE-HOUSES, AND HE'S GETTING A ONE-WAY TICKET TO FABULOUS CLUB FED?!?

BEFORE I GET A CHANCE TO CUT HIS HEART OUT?!?

GORDON'LL KEEP HIM AT GOTHAM CENTRAL 'TIL THE G-MEN COME FOR HIM--THAT I'M SURE OF.

WHICH MEANS IF I WANNA KILL HIM...

YOU COMING UP WITH A PLAN, BOSS?

BLAM BLAM BLAM BLAM

62

Maxie played his part well.

I'll suggest leniency at his sentencing. Thirty years instead of life.

Either way, it's win-win: he'll likely die of old age behind bars, and "Chuckles" manufacturing is shut down for good.

A little less poison on the streets and one less madman to worry about.

Now all I have to do is wait for phase two to kick in.

I figured the televised heavy police presence would keep him from trying to get in on the ground floor.

Which left only one way for him to get to Zeus, if he wanted him bad enough.

And I KNEW he'd want Zeus bad enough.

A doctor at Arkham once described for me the Joker's state of mind.

"Imagine trying to solve the world's most difficult math equation..."

"While you're surrounded by six televisions that sit five inches from your face..."

"All tuned to different stations..."

"All rapidly switching channels..."

"All with the volume at full blast."

"That's what it's like to be the Joker."

You'd think that'd make the Joker an unfathomable foe, impossible to figure out.

But for a capricious, homicidal psychopath with off-the-charts attention deficit disorder...

batman::cacophony #3 *cover by* ADAM KUBERT

THUD

A *HEAD* SHOT?!

FLOMMP

FLOMMP.

I MAKE A TOTAL *SHMUCK* OUT OF MYSELF PLAYIN' IT ALL "ACE OF KNAVES/HARLEQUIN OF HATE"—*OLD SCHOOL*...

I EVEN GO SO FAR AS TO LET *LURCH* THINK *HE'S* USING *ME* TO GET TO *YOU*...

AND YOU DON'T EVEN HAVE THE COMMON *DECENCY* TO SHOOT HIM IN THE *SHOULDER* OR *LEG* SO I CAN FIRE THE *KILL-SHOT MYSELF?*

UHN...
UHN...

Head still ringing, but it'll pass.

Leg's killing me too, but it was worth it.

Knew I could count on the Joker to BE the Joker.

But I owe a bigger thanks to Floyd Lawton.

I "borrowed" Deadshot's helmet technology: the secondary armor beneath the Kevlar headpiece, the blood pack liner for that Grand Guignol effect.

Hate to adopt one of THEIR innovations, but hell...

A good idea's a good idea.

WE'VE BEEN RUNNING THE SAME PATTERN FOR SOME TIME NOW: YOU DO SOMETHING HORRIBLE, I TRACK YOU DOWN, YOU FIGHT ME DIRTY, I TAKE YOU BACK TO ARKHAM.

MY INNER EAR IS SO *ITCHY*...

BUT DURING THIS RARE OPPORTUNITY IN WHICH YOU'RE NOT ONLY PHYSICALLY RESTRAINED, BUT ALSO MOMENTARILY PSYCHOLOGICALLY BALANCED, I FIGURE THIS IS THE BEST TIME TO GET SOME SOUL-SEARCHING *TRUTH* OUT OF YOU.

SO I'M HERE TO ASK YOU...

DO YOU *REALLY* WANT ME DEAD?

DO YOU *REALLY* WANT TO KILL ME?

I DUNNO. LEMME ROLL IT OVER A LITTLE BIT.

MEANTIME, SAME QUESTION APPLIES TO YOU, SPOOKY: YOU WANNA SEE ME DEAD?

I USED TO THINK I'D BE OKAY WITH YOU DYING OR GETTING KILLED, SO LONG AS IT WASN'T BY *MY* HAND OR THE HANDS OF ANY OF MY *ASSOCIATES*.

WHEN YOU SKY-DIVED ONTO THE ROOF OF GOTHAM CENTRAL, I FANTASIZED ABOUT YOUR 'CHUTE MALFUNCTIONING AND YOU PANCAKING ONTO A CURB SOMEWHERE IN THE MIDDLE OF THE CITY.

BUT IN THE MOMENT OF TRUTH, WITH THAT KNIFE STICKING OUT OF YOUR CHEST?

I COULDN'T DO IT. I COULDN'T LET YOU DIE.

FOR ALL THE TRUE EVIL YOU'VE DONE, THE LIVES YOU'VE RUINED, AND THE PAIN YOU'VE INFLICTED, I COULDN'T JUST STAND THERE AND WATCH YOU BLEED OUT--EVEN THOUGH I KNEW IT MEANT GIVING UP A KIND OF PEACE I'VE NEVER KNOWN BEFORE. A KIND OF PEACE I'LL *NEVER* KNOW.

WHY, DO YOU THINK? WHY NOT JUST *ENJOY* THE ULTIMATE VICTORY?

I'VE WATCHED PEOPLE DIE BEFORE.

I SWORE THEN: NEVER AGAIN.

THE CAVE...

WELL, I CAN'T SAY I'M *SURPRISED* BY WHAT THE JOKER SAID, MASTER BRUCE...

IT'S LITTLE WONDER HE *CAUGHT* THAT GLIMPSE, CONSIDERING YOU WEAR YOUR BRIEFS ON THE *OUTSIDE* OF YOUR CLOTHES.

FUNNY.

WELL, I'VE ALWAYS *DREAMED* OF BECOMING A NIGHTCLUB COMIC.

SO DID *HE*.

THE CLOWN'S NOT GONNA STOP 'TIL ONE OF US IS DEAD.

CERTAINLY THIS COMES AS NO SHOCK, MASTER BRUCE.

IT'S JUST... I HELD HIS LIFE IN MY HANDS. GORDON URGED ME TO LET THE JOKER BLEED OUT.

FROM WHAT HE TOLD ME TONIGHT, THAT WOULD'VE GIVEN HIM PEACE.

"DOES HE KNOW THERE'S NO PLACE HE CAN HIDE...

THE END

Here's the script for the first draft of issue three. Compare it against the final comic and you'll see I was able to redeem myself for some eyebrow-raising dialogue ("Nothing to say now, murderer?" is the one that makes ME cringe). Thank God for last-minute dialogue polishes (and editors who'll make it happen, even though the book's about to print). However, page five was so offensive in a completely different way (over-the-top Joker dialogue) that we opted to remove it entirely from the printed issue. You'll notice its absence from the script that follows, as well: that's how off-color that bit was. Best we never speak of it again.

Anyway, peep the first draft. See what a difference the right dialogue and narration makes?

Batman: Cacophony

Part Three:

Baffles

By

Kevin Smith

EXT GOTHAM CENTRAL ROOFTOP - NIGHT

Panel One

A reverse of the last panel of issue two. Foreground: we're
over Onomatopoeia, waist-down, guns at his sides as they were
at end of last ish. In the mid/background, it's Batman
standing defensively, Joker happy, still cuffed to
the Bat signal, shattered glass from the Bat signal
in evidence on ground around him.

Panel Two

Close on Batman, chest-up.

                    BATMAN INTERNAL 1
          You've got him, Bruce.

                    BATMAN INTERNAL 2
          He's no match for your years of
          training.

Panel Three

A corresponding close on Ono, chest-up.

                    BATMAN INTERNAL
          Those guns are his only edge.

Panel Four

Insert panel: tight on Joker's hand grabbing a particularly
nasty, large shard of broken Bat signal glass; big enough to
be used as a weapon.

                    BATMAN INTERNAL (CONT'D)
          Even from this distance, you've got
          him...

Panel Five

The Joker madly swinging glass piece through the air, in
overhead arch.

                    BATMAN INTERNAL (CONT'D)
          Barring any *unseen* variables.

Panel Six

The Joker maniacally plunging the glass shard into Batman's
calf, with Batman reacting.

                    JOKER
          SHOOT HIM NOW! SHOOT HIM NOW!

Panel Seven

Ono immediately throws up right gun-hand and fires.

                    SFX
          BLAM!

PAGES TWO AND THREE

Splash Page:

Ono in the background, smoking gun pointed at Batman, who's
in the foreground, back sort of to us; but Bats' upper torso
is twisted toward us from the impact of the shot: right into
his cowl's forehead. Blood spraying everywhere. The Joker
is delighted. It would appear that Batman's been shot dead
through his skull. The air is filled with the Joker's
HAHAHAHAHAHAHA.

                    BATMAN
          UHN!

                    CREDITS
          Batman: Cacophony
          Part 3: Baffles
          Writer: Kevin Smith
          Artist: Walt Flanagan
          Inker: Sandra Hope
          Colorist: Guy Major
          Lettering:
          Editor: Dan DiDio
          Covers: Kubert
          Batman created by Bob Kane

PAGE FOUR

Panel One

Batman falling onto his back on the rooftop, apparently dead,
blood pouring from his head-shot.

                    SFX
                (body hitting ground)
          THUD!

Panel Two

Onomatopoeia leaps into the air from his doorway perch.

Panel Three

Close on Ono's feet hitting the deck in the foreground,
some dust rising from the impact. In the back and mid ground,
the Batman is laying dead on the rooftop, out of the Joker's
reach. The Joker is beyond delighted.

                  SFX (CONT'D)
      FLOMMMP!

Panel Four

Ono, standing now, as if he'd landed with buckled knees.

                ONOMATOPOEIA
      Flommmp.

Panel Five

The Joker's desperately trying to reach the out-of-reach
Batman, but he's still cuffed to Bat signal.

                JOKER
      Uhn! Can't... reach...
          (balloon two)
      Listen here, Chatty-Kathy: can
      you... uhn... get me out of these
      cuffs...

PAGE SIX

Panel One

Chest-up on Ono, who now brings his bloody gun up, pointing
it at the off-panel Joker. Batman's unseen, below the bottom
of the frame.

Panel Two

The Joker reacting to the gun pointing at him. Ono's not in the
frame; just his pointing gun coming in from the right side of
the panel.

                JOKER (CONT'D)
      Um... no sweat, Buddy.

Panel Three

Same set-up, but now Batman's hand has thrust up into the
frame, violently grabbing Ono's gun hand and snapping the
wrist. The Joker's gone wide-eyed.

                    SFX
          KRR-SNAP!

Panel Four

Ono reeling back, in pain, with snapped wrist, bringing other
gun hand around to shoot.

                    ONOMATOPOEIA
          AAAHHHHHHH!

Panel Five

Close on Bats' foot coming up (from where it was laying on
the roof) kicking Ono's other gun from his other hand. It's
firing as it's kicked, but the shot hits nothing, thanks to
the kick-block.

                    SFX
          KICK!

                    SFX (CONT'D)
          BLAM!

Panel Six

Close on Ono getting punched in the face by Batman's fist.

                    SFX (CONT'D)
          KEE-RUNCH!

                    ONOMATOPOEIA
          UHNFF!

PAGE SEVEN

Panel One

Ono on his butt, holding his snapped wrist to his chest, his
eye-line following the off-panel Batman, who's presumably
standing up. There's some rain starting to hit the roof.

                    ONOMATOPOEIA (CONT'D)
          Uhn... Uhn...

                    BATMAN INTERNAL
          Head still ringing, but it'll pass.

Panel Two

The Joker, looking scared, his eye-line following the off-panel
Batman, who's presumably standing up. More rain now; it's
getting heavier.

> BATMAN INTERNAL 1
> All I had to do was stand within
> striking distance of the clown and
> count on the Joker to *be* the Joker.

> BATMAN INTERNAL 2
> But I owe a bigger thanks to Floyd
> Lawton.

Panel Three

Biggest panel on the page: Batman standing over the grounded
Onomatopoeia (his back sort of to us). Lightning strikes
behind him far off in the distance. It's now raining full
out, from here on in.

> BATMAN INTERNAL 1
> I "borrowed" Deadshot's helmet
> technology: the secondary armor
> beneath the Kevlar headpiece, the
> blood pack liner for that Grand
> Guignol effect.

> BATMAN INTERNAL 2
> Normally, I prefer any innovations
> I incorporate to be my own, but
> hell...

> BATMAN INTERNAL 3
> A good idea's a good idea.

PAGE EIGHT

Panel One

Close on Batman's hand violently grabbing Onomatopoeia by his
snapped wrist.

> BATMAN INTERNAL
> And I just had *another* one...

> ONOMATOPOEIA
> AAAHHHHH!!!

Panel Two

Batman yanks Ono to his feet with one hand, and pulls back
with the other.

Panel Three

Batman punching Ono something fierce in the face, throwing
him backwards.

                    SFX
          KRAK!

Panel Four

Ono on the ground, throws a sweep kick across the ground
at Batman's feet, but Batman leaps into the air in place,
causing Ono to miss.

                    SFX (CONT'D)
                 (missed leg sweep)
          WIFFFF!

Panel Five

Ono's kinda facing us in an upward-dog position. Batman comes
down from his hop-up, landing on Ono's calf hard, with a...

                    SFX (CONT'D)
          SNAP!

                    ONOMATOPOEIA
          UHNNN!

PAGE NINE

Panel One

The Joker, seeing all this happening off-panel, reacts with
a "I was with you the whole time"-kinda caught expression,
desperately trying to get his hand out of the Bat cuff at
the same time.

                    JOKER
          Uh... yeah. Get him, Bats.
               (balloon two)
          I knew you were going for that...
          uh... *playing possum* thing - which
          is the reason... the *ONLY* reason I
          pretended to stab you in the leg,
          see?
               (balloon three)
          For reals.

Panel Two

Tight on Ono's face being punched hard by a downward blow
from Batman's fist.

                         SFX
              SOK!

                         BATMAN INTERNAL
              I shut out the clown's rambling and
              make a meal out of this mask-
              killer.

Panel Three

Batman picking up Ono by his collar, lifting him off the
ground so he's over Bats.

                         BATMAN INTERNAL 1
              This is for Buckeye.

                         BATMAN INTERNAL 2
              And Virago.

                         BATMAN INTERNAL 3
              And who knows how many other would-
              be heroes you've stalked and
              killed.

Panel Four

Close on Batman, teeth gritted, looking up at Ono's face.

                         BATMAN
              Nothing to say *now*, murderer?
                    (balloon two)
              Lemme help you out with that...

Panel Five

Batman, post-punch (in body language); Ono flying at us.

                         SFX
              POW!

Panel One

The beaten Ono, landing beside the still-cuffed Joker, who
reacts terrified.

                    SFX (CONT'D)
          KA-THUD!

                    JOKER
          Man alive - did I hitch *my* wagon to
          the wrong star.

Panel Two

With the close Joker looking on, Ono struggles to roll over,
reaching into his coat.

                    JOKER (CONT'D)
          Or maybe not...
                    (balloon two; smaller;
                    whispering)
          Get it, buddy! Let's book a trip
          to that Last Resort!

Panel Three

Ono has pulled his massive hunting knife from his coat,
brandishing it weakly, as the Joker excitedly looks on,
cheering. The Joker is reaching into his own coat with
his free hand now.

                    JOKER (CONT'D)
          Now we're talking! Yes!

Panel Four

Over the raised knife-holding hand in the foreground, onto
Bats reacting in the mid-to-background.

                    OFF-PANEL JOKER
          Eat it, Bats! We're gonna put *real*
          holes in your dumb ass now!

Panel Five

Ono, sitting up sorta now, beside the yelling Joker, who
waves a small cheerleader pom-pom with his free hand.

                    JOKER
          Gut that *pig*! *Bury* that sweet
          steel into his *sanctimonious*...

Panel One

Biggest panel on the page: Ono plunges the knife into the
Joker's heart. The Joker reacts wide-eyed. Blood shoots out
everywhere. (Guy: can you do that motion effect on Ono's
knife-hand that you did for ish one, when Bats punched
through the wall to get to Zsasz? Thanks.)

                        SFX
             SHHHUNTTTTT!!!

                        JOKER
                   (weakly; small)
             Heart?

Panel Two

Close on Batman reacting.

                        BATMAN INTERNAL
             No!

Panel Three

Ono hurls himself atop the knife, pushing it deeper. The
Joker's in agony, spitting up blood. Batman's racing toward
them.

                        SFX
             SQUISH-UNT!

                        JOKER
             AAAAAAARRRRRGGGGHHHHHH!!!

Panel Four

Batman pulls Ono off the Joker, throwing him backwards. The
knife is buried to the hilt in the Joker's chest.

                        BATMAN INTERNAL 1
             Not *tonight*!

                        BATMAN INTERNAL 2
             Not on *my* watch!

Panel Five

Batman is pressing down around the wound, trying to stop the
bleeding. Joker's losing consciousness.

                    BATMAN INTERNAL 1
          He buried the knife so deeply, I
          can't risk extracting it, 'lest the
          Clown bleed out.

                    BATMAN INTERNAL 2
          Applying pressure around the wound
          to stop the bleeding, but he's a
          geyser at this point.

                    BATMAN INTERNAL 3
          On top of this, I have to worry
          about second attack from...

PAGE TWELVE

Panel One

Over Ono's arm and mangled wrist/hand that he's holding with
his free hand (but we're over his back). Batman's kneeling
at the Joker's side in profile, applying pressure to the
knife-wound, looking at us/Ono.

                    BATMAN INTERNAL 1
          Oh.

                    BATMAN INTERNAL 2
          I get it.

Panel Two

Corresponding over: Over Bat's (in profile), his head facing
Ono - who stands at the roof's edge, beside the roof exit,
"looking" at us, beaten, battered, clothes and mask torn
and bloody.

                    BATMAN INTERNAL
          Stabbing the Joker wasn't a
          diversion.

                    BATMAN INTERNAL 2
          It's a *test*.

Panel Three

Close on Batman. Still raining, don't forget.

> BATMAN INTERNAL
> It's a test of my *code*.

> BATMAN INTERNAL 2
> Save the life of someone whose very
> existence jeopardizes the lives of
> others...

Panel Four

Close on the beaten, slightly-hunched Ono - waiting.

> BATMAN INTERNAL
> Or stop someone whose very
> existence jeopardizes the lives of
> others...

> BATMAN INTERNAL 2
> As well as my own.

Panel Five

Over (meaning overhead, in this instance), Batman, looking
down on the bleeding-out, dying Joker. We should be looking
straight down. Rain pouring all around them; puddles.

> BATMAN INTERNAL
> I know what I *should* do...

> BATMAN INTERNAL 2
> I just *can't*.

PAGE THIRTEEN

Panel One

This panel is a mirror of panel two on the last page, only
now, Ono's not where he was standing in that panel; he's
completely vanished.

> BATMAN INTERNAL
> God help me, I just *can't*...

Panel Two

Same set-up as the previous panel, but in the foreground,
Batman's scooping up the Joker. In the background, the
stairwell door is being kicked open by Gordon and some
armed/armored Cops.

                    SFX
          SLAM!

                    GORDON
          What *happened*?! Where *is* he?!

Panel Three

Biggest panel on the page: Batman, standing in the rain,
holding the dying, unconscious Joker in his arms. Blood
and water run down his body, puddling on the rooftop.

                    BATMAN
          He stabbed the Joker, Jim.
          Through the *heart*.
                    (balloon two)
          He's *dying*.

PAGE FOURTEEN

Panel One

High overhead of the Cops fanning out, guns and rifles raised
defensively, looking for anyone else on the roof. Gordon
approaches the Joker-holding Batman.

                    GORDON
          Where's the *other* guy? The *Mask—*
          killer?

                    BATMAN
          He escaped.

                    GORDON
          You're not going *after* him?

                    BATMAN
          I've got to deal with the Joker.

                    GORDON
          What're you *talking* about?!

                    BATMAN
          Jim - if I don't get him medical
          attention immediately, he'll die.

Panel Two

Over Bats' shoulder, onto Gordon. Gordon's glaring at the
off-panel Batman. In the background, the Cops, looking
around. The stairwell is in evidence in the background.

Panel Three

Same set-up, but now the Cops in the background are reacting
to Gordon - who's calling back over his shoulder a bit, still
holding his look to Batman (whose face we still can't see).

> GORDON
> I want everyone to *stand down*!
> > (balloon two)
> Off this roof! *NOW*!

Panel Four

Same set-up, but the Cops in the background are heading
toward the stairwell exit. Gordon's looking back over his
shoulder slightly, to make sure the other Cops are leaving.

Panel Five

Same set-up, but now the Cops are all gone. Gordon's looking
at Batman again; glaring, really.

> GORDON (CONT'D)
> Are you *crazy*?
> > (balloon two)
> *Let* him die!

PAGE FIFTEEN

Panel One

Close on Batman, chest-up; surprised.

> BATMAN
> I... I *can't*, Jim.
> > (balloon two)
> It was *my* idea to use him as *bait*.
> *I* got him stabbed.

Panel Two

An angry Gordon gives Batman an earful.

> GORDON
> *No!*
>   (balloon two)
> What got him *stabbed* was his
> fundamental inability to ever be
> anything but *evil incarnate*!

> BATMAN
> Jim...

> GORDON
> Don't *"Jim"* me! He's a *monster* and
> you *know* it!

> BATMAN
> We can't let ourselves forget that
> he's a *human being* too!

> GORDON
> Oh yes we can! Think about all the
> *horror* he's wreaked in this city -
> for longer than I can *remember*!

Panel Three

Biggest panel on the page. A flashback of the Joker's
greatest hits, so to speak: random people clutching at their
own throats, their faces constricting in rictus grins; the
shooting of Barbara Gordon; the torturing of Jim Gordon
(Killing Joke); the beating of Jason Todd; anything else
you can think of, include. Maybe throw in Batman's head
into the middle or something, as if all these images are
swirling around in it. Your call.

> GORDON VOICEOVER
> Think about what he's done to the
> *people* in this city...

> GORDON VOICEOVER 2
> Think about what he did to *me*...

> GORDON VOICEOVER 3
> What he did to *Barbara*...

> GORDON VOICEOVER 4
> What he's done to *you*!

Panel One

Close on the face of the Joker in Batman's arms, hanging
back and lolling down. The water running down his rain soaked
face is mixed with blood; his hair, now soaked, is long, the
water pulling it toward the ground. Leave enough space for
all the off-panel Gordon's word balloons.

> GORDON
> I understood why you never killed
> him *yourself*: you've got a moral
> code I've respected for *years*.
> (balloon two)
> But I'm not asking you to *kill* him
> here...
> (balloon three)
> I'm just asking you not to *save* his
> worthless, *corrosive* life!
> (balloon four)
> You didn't *do* this. You didn't
> *stab* him. This is *his* doing.
> (balloon five)
> He made his choices.

Panel Two

INT STAIRWELL - SAME

We're in the stairwell, over the armored cops (who'd been on
the roof), hiding in the shadows at the top of the stairwell,
watching this scene play out in the distance.

> BATMAN
> He can't *make* choices, Jim.
> (balloon two)
> He's *insane*.

> GORDON
> *Insanity* would be keeping him
> *alive*, so he can drop *another*
> building on *another* bunch of *school
> kids*!

Panel Three

Close on Gordon.

                    GORDON (CONT'D)
          Do the right thing here. For
          Gotham's sake.
                    (balloon two)
          For *your* sake.
                    (balloon three)
          Let him *go*.

Panel Four

A profile of Batman holding the dying Joker in his arms,
as Jim Gordon looks at him pleadingly. The rain falls.

Panel Five

Same shot, but pulled away more (so the figures are
about 40% smaller, and we're seeing more of the roof/
surrounding buildings.

Panel Six

Same shot, but now pulled back even further, so Batman
(holding dying Joker) and Gordon are very tiny figures.

PAGE SEVENTEEN

Panel One

INT HOSPITAL HALLWAY - NIGHT

We're at one end of a long corridor, at the other end of
which stand two armed (with rifles) and armored Police.
They guard a pair of what look like supermarket entry doors
marked with the huge letters I.C.U. There's no bustle in the
hallway as with most hospitals; the whole floor's empty,
except for the armored guards, who're tiny in the distance.
Throw a few pieces of hospital equipment into the hallway,
though - just to nail our location home for the reader.

Panel Two

Same exact shot, but now a LAWYER is walking down the hallway
(back to us), carrying a briefcase, heading for the I.C.U.
Give him curly, fro-ish hair.

Panel Three

Same exact shot, but now the LAWYER is in front of the
armored guards, holding up a few pieces of paper that're
stapled together. The guards look at the paper.

                    LAWYER
          Gentlemen, I'm from the firm of
          Malone & Malone. We've been
          retained to represent the patient.
          I understand he came out of his
          coma this morning. As his
          attorney, I'm entitled to speak to
          him.
                    (balloon two)
          This is a court order from a
          circuit judge saying as much -
          guaranteeing me undisturbed, un-
          monitored face-time with my client.

PAGE EIGHTEEN

Panel One

Close on the Joker, in a hospital bed, his face buried in Ayn
Rand's "The Fountainhead." His hair is visibly longer now.
He's hooked up to an I.V. unit. There are restraints around
his arms, wrists, chest - everywhere, really. He's got just
enough slack to read his book. In the foreground, we see a
shoulder of the Lawyer.

Panel Two

Same image, but now the Joker has lowered the book slightly,
to take in his guest. He looks like utter crap: like he's
been out for months. Maybe give him a green, straggly beard.

Panel Three

The Joker goes back to reading his book.

                    JOKER
          'lo, Bats.

Panel Four

The first time we're seeing the face of MATCHES MALONE
(aka, Bruce Wayne in disguise, a matchstick jutting out of
the corner of his mouth). He stands at the Joker's bedside.
His briefcase is placed on one of those wheeled hospital
tables that patients use.

                    MATCHES
          Joker.

Panel One

The Joker continues reading his book. Matches looks on.

                    JOKER
          I'm glad to see you haven't garaged
          the old *disguise kit*.
                    (balloon two)
          Matches strikes again.

                    MATCHES
          Cute.

Panel Two

Joker tosses his book to the side.

                    JOKER
                    (smaller; as if a sotto aside)
          I'm *never* gonna finish this book...
                    (balloon two; regular size)
          To what do I owe this unexpected
          pleasure?

Panel Three

Matches looking down at the Joker in bed.

                    MATCHES
          Just checking up on you.
                    (balloon two)
          I'm sure they already let you know
          you've been in a coma for five
          months now.

                    JOKER
          Ayup. Now they've got me *doped up*
          on *morphine* - not to mention an *ass-
          load* of mood stabilizers and anti-
          psychotics.

                    MATCHES
          That's why I'm here. I couldn't
          pass up the opportunity to have a
          somewhat *rational* conversation with
          you.

Panel Four

The Joker offering a sheepish grin.

                    OFF-PANEL MATCHES
          Or, at least, a conversation during
          which you're not trying to poison
          me, hit me with that hammer, or
          feed me to killer fish.

                    JOKER
          It's what I *do*.

PAGE TWENTY

Panel One

Matches turns his back to the Joker and looks out
the curtained window. The Joker is rolling his eyes.

                    MATCHES
          We've only ever had one other
          chance to do this: after *Luthor* put
          together that bid to destroy the
          League with a "corporate takeover."
                    (balloon two)
          The Martian telepathically ordered
          your thought patterns into
          something resembling a brief state
          of *sanity*.

                    JOKER
          I don't know what you're talking
          about, but I'm telling you right
          now: I can't take you *seriously* in
          that *get-up*.
                    (balloon two)
          I'm guessing your *real* face is in
          that briefcase?

Panel Two

Matches holds his briefcase in one hand, and closes a curtain
(the kind hung from the ceiling around a patient's bed in the
hospital; a privacy curtain) with his other hand - as if he's
gonna get dressed.

                             MATCHES
            It is.

                             JOKER
            Well strap it on, then. That
            mustache is creeping me out.

Panel Three

On the Joker, strapped into bed.

                        JOKER (CONT'D)
            So, the last thing I *remember* was
            you Costner-ing me in your arms
            like I was *Whitney Houston*, while
            you *argued* with the right reverend
            Gordon about the *merits* of keeping me
            from slipping loose this mortal coil.
                (balloon two)
            Naturally, if I'd had *any* strength
            whatsoever, I'd have bitten into
            your *jugular* while you were
            cradling *me* in your lovin' arms.
                (balloon three)
            But considering how it all worked
            out, I guess I should just say
            "thanks."

Panel Four

Batman, now fully dressed in his gear, slides the curtain
open.

                        BATMAN
            You're welcome.
                (balloon two)
            Which brings me to my question...

Panel One

On the Joker, trying to scratch his ear by rubbing his head
on the pillow (since his hands are restrained).

> OFF-PANEL BATMAN
> We've been doing this for some time
> now: you do something horrible, I
> track you down, you fight me
> viciously, I take you back to Arkham.

> JOKER
> My inner ear is so *itchy*...

> OFF-PANEL BATMAN
> But during this rare opportunity in
> which you're not only physically
> restrained, but also momentarily
> psychologically balanced, I figure
> this is the best time to get some
> soul-searching *truth* out of you.

Panel Two

Close on Batman.

> BATMAN
> So I'm here to ask you...
>> (balloon two; it should be
>> more distant from balloon
>> one - as if he's giving a
>> pregnant pause)
> Do you *really* want me dead?
>> (balloon three)
> Do you *really* want to kill me?

Panel Three

Close on the Joker, mulling that thought over. Remember,
he's drugged-up, so his expression can't be too crazy. He
should look like a six year old trying to solve a math
equation.

Panel Four

Same set-up, but now the Joker opens his mouth to speak.

> JOKER
> I dunno. Lemme roll it over a little bit.
> (balloon two)
> Meantime, same question applies to
> you, Spooky: you wanna see me dead?

PAGE TWENTY TWO

Panel One

Long panel going down the left side. All Batman.

> BATMAN
> I used to think I was okay with you
> dying or getting killed, so long as
> it wasn't by *my* hand or the hands
> of any of my *associates*.
> (balloon two)
> When you sky-dived onto the roof of
> Gotham Central, I fantasized about
> your 'chute malfunctioning and you
> pancaking onto a curb somewhere in
> the middle of the city.
> (balloon three)
> But in the moment of truth, with
> that knife sticking out of your chest?

Panel Two

Batman looking down, ashamed sort of. The Joker takes this in.

> BATMAN (CONT'D)
> I couldn't do it. I couldn't let
> you die.
> (balloon two)
> For all the true evil you've done,
> the lives you've ruined, and the
> pain you've inflicted, I couldn't
> just stand there and watch you
> bleed out - even though I knew it
> meant giving up a kind of peace
> I've never known before. A kind of
> peace I'll never know.

> JOKER
> *Why*, do you think? Why not just
> *enjoy* the ultimate victory?

Panel Three

Close on Batman, looking momentarily forlorn. Over his shoulder (or around him) we see ghostly images of the gun muzzle, the pearl necklace breaking, and the young Bruce kneeling on the ground between his dead parents.

                    BATMAN
          I've watched people die before.
               (balloon two)
          I swore then: never again.

PAGE TWENTY THREE

Panel One

Wider on Batman now. He holds his cape out a bit, examining himself - as if he's saying, "Look at all this..."

                    BATMAN (CONT'D)
          My whole life... all of *this*.
               (balloon two)
          It's all because I never want to
          see death first-hand again.

Panel Two

Joker, in bed, restrained.

                    JOKER
          Interesting. I always *thought*
          your misguided sense of self-
          righteousness came from some
          personal tragedy.
               (balloon two)
          I'm sorry for whatever it was that
          happened to you which made you the
          way you are.

Panel Three

Close on Batman.

                    BATMAN
          Thank you.

Panel Four

Close on Joker.

                    JOKER
          But I *do* want to kill you.

Panel Five

On Batman, who barely reacts.

PAGE TWENTY FOUR

Panel One

The Joker.

                    JOKER (CONT'D)
          I imagine that's hard to hear,
          after you just opened yourself
          up to me like you did.
                    (balloon two)
          I imagine, in your head, you saw
          this visit as a chance to work on
          the nature of our relationship
          while I'm temporarily *not* a
          frothing-at-the-mouth, raving
          lunatic.
                    (balloon three)
          You probably saw this visit as a
          chance for a *new* beginning.

Panel Two

Closer on the Joker.

                    JOKER (CONT'D)
          But here's the cold, hard truth, Bats...
                    (balloon two)
          I don't hate you 'cause I'm crazy...

Panel Three

Even closer on the Joker.

                    JOKER (CONT'D)
          I'm crazy 'cause I hate you.

Panel Four

On Batman.

> OFF-PANEL JOKER
> And your death - preferably, but
> not necessarily, by my hand - will
> represent the end of my reign of
> terror in this city. In this world.
> (balloon two)
> When you're gone, I'll stop hurting
> people I don't know. I'll stop
> with the mayhem and murder.
> (balloon three)
> I'll lock myself up in a hospital
> and run out my clock staring at the
> walls, hopped up on premium grade
> *pharmaceuticals* that leave me so
> virtually *lobotomized*, they'll have
> to catheterize and colostomize my
> holes to keep me from becoming a
> non-stop self-pissing and pooping
> *mess*.

PAGE TWENTY FIVE

Panel One

On the Joker again.

> JOKER
> I can tell by your face that I've
> disappointed you.
> (balloon two)
> But you're a big, strong guy who's
> obviously familiar with
> disappointment and disillusionment,
> so I'm thinking you can handle this
> information...

Panel Two

Closer on the Joker, smiling.

> JOKER (CONT'D)
> Yes, I *want* to kill you.
> (balloon two)
> And one day, I'm *going* to kill you.
> (balloon three)
> And then?
> (balloon four)
> Then we'll *both* finally be free.

Panel Three

Batman standing near Joker's bedside. The pair don't really look at one another. They just dwell in the moment.

Panel Four

Same.

Panel Five

Same, but now the Joker speaks.

> JOKER (CONT'D)
> Since we're being super truthful,
> I should also tell you I saw a little
> bit of your junk when you were
> getting changed before.

PAGE TWENTY SIX

INT BAT CAVE

Panel One

Wide on a section of the cave we haven't seen previously in our book: Bruce hangs his cape and cowl in a vault-like single suit closet. Alfred is standing nearby with a laundry basket.

> CAPTION
> The Cave...

> ALFRED
> Well I can't say I'm *surprised* by
> what the Joker said, Master
> Bruce...

Panel Two

Closer now. Bruce pulls off his shirt. Alfred dutifully stands by, waiting for the laundry.

> ALFRED (CONT'D)
> It's little wonder he caught a
> glimpse, since you wear your briefs
> on the *outside* of your clothes.

> BRUCE
> Funny.

Panel Three

Wide again. The shirt's in the laundry basket, and Bruce is pulling on a robe. Some bats fly by in the foreground.

> ALFRED
> Well, I've always *dreamed* of becoming a nightclub comic.

> BRUCE
> I now know for sure: the Clown won't stop 'til I'm dead.

> ALFRED
> Certainly this comes as no shock, Master Bruce.

> BRUCE
> It's just... I held his life in my hands. Gordon urged me to let the Joker bleed out.
> (balloon two)
> From what he told me tonight, that would've given him peace.

PAGE TWENTY SEVEN

Panel One

Another wide shot from a different angle. Bruce now tosses his leggings and Bat-shorts into the laundry basket Alfred holds.

> ALFRED
> Some men and women want to change the *world*, so they run for office. Some men and women want to change *themselves*, so they study and meditate.
> (balloon two)
> The only difference between you and those people is the fundamentals with which you and they enact that change.
> (balloon three)
> Those people take a more *traditional* route to implement the changes they want to see. *You?* You find it easier to put on these clothes and hurl yourself into the path of danger and death on a nightly basis to realize the changes you seek.

Panel Two

INT STUDY

Bruce and Alfred emerge from the secret passageway into the
Bat cave: a hidden door in a massive wall of bookshelves.

                    BRUCE
          I don't make it *easy* on myself, do I?

                    ALFRED
          Or anybody else, for that matter.
          But that's what makes you *you*,
          Master Bruce: the path of least
          resistance has never been your
          preferred course.

Panel Three

INT LIVING ROOM

Massive. Huge, man-sized fireplace, lit. Bruce and
Alfred very small, walking through it.

                    ALFRED (CONT'D)
          Still no sign of the *other* fellow,
          then? The upstanding citizen with
          the penchant for onomatopoetics?

                    BRUCE
          None.
               (balloon two)
          It follows the pattern of his Star
          City activities from a few years
          back: he goes after a big gun,
          fails, then shrinks back into
          the darkness.

Panel Four

Alfred in the foreground, about to pass out of the panel.
Bruce behind him.

                    ALFRED
          Even monsters need their rest, I suppose.

                    BRUCE
          I just wish I knew more about him...

Panel One

EXT SUBURBAN STREET - DAY

Wide (across the street) on a taxi cab idling in front of
a modest two story house, complete with white picket fence.
A MAN is climbing out of the cab, carrying a briefcase. We
don't see both of his arms, though. There are other houses
on the block, in the yards of which normal things are
happening: lawn mowing, kids playing, joggers jogging.

                    BRUCE VOICE-OVER
               Where does he go when he's not
               hunting heroes?

Panel Two

Over the roof of the cab, we're on the back of the Man
emerging from the cab in the foreground. In the background,
we see a FAMILY emerging from the house: Mother, seven and
eight year old daughter and son. Even a dog. They're all
wearing excited smiles.

                    BRUCE VOICE-OVER (CONT'D)
               Who are his confidants? His
               henchmen?

Panel Three

The cab's pulling away. In the yard, the kids are hugging
the Dad's legs, as the Dad kisses the Mom (thus hiding his
face). There are two suitcases in evidence, sitting beside
them, as well as the Man's briefcase.

                    BRUCE VOICE-OVER (CONT'D)
               Does he maintain dual identities,
               or is he this murderous creature
               all the time?

Panel Four

The Mom studies/holds what appears to be a cast on the Dad's
forearm and wrist. She wears a concerned expression. The
man holds up a broken tennis racket, indicating the source
of his wrist injury. We still don't see his face.

                    BRUCE VOICE-OVER (CONT'D)
               How does he live above suspicion?

Panel One

INT HOUSE - DAY

The son and daughter carry the bags in the front door in the
background, and the Man (cut off at the shoulders by the top
of the panel) looks through some mail on a table. The Mom is
hanging his top coat on a coat hanger by the door.

> BRUCE VOICE-OVER (CONT'D)
> Does he spend every waking hour
> plotting his next kill, or does he
> have a life *outside* of death?

Panel Two

INT BASEMENT STAIRWELL

The Man is descending the stairs, his back to us, looking up
at his wife, who's in the doorway at the top of the stairs,
stirring a pot she's holding. The man holds his briefcase
up, indicating some work to be done downstairs.

> BRUCE VOICE-OVER (CONT'D)
> How does he reconcile *what* he does
> to *who* he is?

Panel Three

INT BASEMENT

Pool table, boxes with Christmas decorations, etc. Our man
passes them by, heading toward a bookshelf. We still don't
see his face.

> BRUCE VOICE-OVER (CONT'D)
> And in the wee small hours of the
> morning, when he's alone with his
> thoughts...

Panel Four

Insert: close on man pulling back hinged book in book case.

> BRUCE VOICE-OVER (CONT'D)
> Is he honest with himself?

Panel Five

The book case clicks open, affording us a view of a hidden
room that the Man is entering.

                    BRUCE VOICE-OVER (CONT'D)
               Does he know there's no place he
               can hide from himself?

Panel Six

Close on the Onomatopoeia mask being pulled over a
dummy head. There's some evidence of the bloody battle
with Batman.

                    BRUCE VOICE-OVER (CONT'D)
               Does he know there's no place he
               can hide from justice?

PAGE THIRTY

SPLASH PAGE

Note: the page should be a horizontal splash, not a vertical
one.

It's Onomatopoeia's trophy room/lair. Along a wall are long
shelf-like beams upon which sit domed glass cases. Some have
nothing in them, but others sport domino masks and headpieces
of past kills, along with name-plates to identify them:
Buckeye, Virago (see Green Arrow issues for mask designs).
There are ten other masks for characters we didn't see Ono
kill in comics, but can assume he's been busy: The Strobe,
Phantom Jockey, The Ritz, Sky-Rider, Brawler, Washingtonian,
Lady Justice, Bible Belt, The Ringer, Brother Black. There
are empty jars marked "Blue Beetle", "Steel", "Green Arrow
I", "Green Arrow II", and "Black Canary". The masks in the
glass domes/jars should look like Robin's costume in the
Bat-Cave: seemingly hovering in mid air.

Put some computers in the room, too. Maps of Gotham
pinned to walls with lines indicating prey he's following.
Articles hang, ripped from newspapers, that detail Batman's
many recent busts and activities. There's also an arsenal
of serious firepower: guns of all sizes, as well as
hunting knives.

In the midst of all this, the Man, his back to us, studies a
glass dome for which we can't see the label.

                    BRUCE VOICE-OVER (CONT'D)
              Does he know there's no place he
              can hide...

INSERT PANEL: Close on the glass dome, in his hands, that's
labeled "The Batman."

                    BRUCE VOICE-OVER (CONT'D)
              ...from *me*?

                         THE END

batman::cacophony #1 *variant cover by* BILL SIENKIEWICZ

batman::cacophony #2 *variant cover by* BILL SIENKIEWICZ

batman::cacophony #3 *variant cover by* BILL SIENKIEWICZ

DEADSHOT

• You cool with the 80's version?

• If possible I'd love to Draw FLOYD as well

sketches by WALT FLANAGAN